TIME TRAVELING TO
1974

CELEBRATING A SPECIAL YEAR

TIME TRAVELING TO 1974

Author
James R. Miller

Design
Gonçalo Sousa

November 2023
ISBN: 9798868427626

Surprise!

Dear reader, thank you so much for purchasing my book!

To make this book more (much more!) affordable, the images are all black & white, but I've created a special gift for you!

You can now have access, for FREE, to the PDF version of this book with the original images!

Keep in mind that some are originally black and white, but some are colored.

Go to page 103 and follow the instructions to download it.

I hope you enjoy it!

Contents

Chapter I: News & Current Events 1974

Leading Events

Economic Tremors: The Oil Price Shock - Oct. 1973-Jan. 1974

Automobiles lined up in a double line due to national gas shortages.

In the dramatic autumn of 1973, in a world stage featuring the Yom Kippur War, the Organization of Arab Petroleum Exporting Countries (OAPEC) dramatically pulled the oil rug from beneath the United States, following President Nixon's appeal for $2.2 billion emergency aid for Israel. They slammed the oil door shut with an embargo and cranked up the heat with a series of production cuts. This wasn't just an ordinary price hike - oil prices soared to dizzying heights, leaping from a measly $2.90 a barrel to a whopping $11.65 by the time 1974 dawned.

The United States was already riding an economic roller coaster, juggling soaring prices, industries running at full steam, and a dire scarcity of essential materials. When OAPEC decided to play oil-hardball, the U.S. oil industry was left scrambling, lacking the surplus capacity to satiate the thirsty oil markets. Hence, OAPEC's decisions sent prices skyrocketing.

Add to this simmering stew the rise of the Organization of the Petroleum Exporting Countries (OPEC) who, flexing their growing market share muscles, began to throw their weight around the global oil price ring. Let's not forget the resilient dollar either, which in the early 70s took a nosedive, effectively denting the revenues of OPEC nations. No longer fans

Owner spray paints a sign outside his Phillips 66 station in Perkasie, Pennsylvania

of the plummeting dollar, OPEC nations decided to have a golden affair, pricing their oil in terms of the precious metal. But when the Bretton Woods agreement, which had pegged gold to a price of $35, was tossed out, gold prices rocketed to a breathtaking $455 an ounce by the end of the 70s. This wild roller coaster ride of the dollar's value undeniably played a starring role in the thrilling saga of the oil price increases of the 1970s.

ABBA's 'Waterloo': Eurovision Crowned - April 6th

A pop music sensation emerged from a place more known for its ice-cold winters than its music: Sweden. A band named ABBA, an acronym of the first letters of the members' first names (Agnetha, Bjorn, Benny, and Anni-Frid), won the Eurovision Song Contest with a catchy tune named 'Waterloo.' This victory on the international stage was the catalyst for ABBA's ascent to global stardom.

'Waterloo' was a song that blended elements of pop and rock with the distinctive Nordic sound. The music was infectious, and the lyrics were

ABBA

playful yet powerful, resonating with audiences across Europe and later, the world. The Eurovision Song Contest, more than just a music competition, served as a platform for countries to showcase their musical talents and cultural richness. For ABBA, it was the launching pad to a prolific career that would span decades, influence generations of musicians, and cement their place in pop culture history. ABBA's victory and subsequent global success marked a turning point in the world of music. It highlighted the universal appeal of pop music, transcending borders and cultures, and paved the way for non-English-speaking countries to make significant inroads into the international music scene.

Expo '74: The World's Fair Unveiled - May 4th

On the banks of the Spokane River, in the heart of the Pacific Northwest, the smallest city ever to host a World's Fair welcomed the world. Expo '74, held in Spokane, Washington, was a significant milestone in the city's history and a landmark event on the global stage.

Inside U.S. Pavilion

The fair's theme, 'Celebrating Tomorrow's Fresh New Environment,' was a stark departure from the usual technology-driven themes of past Expos. It reflected the spirit of the era – a flourishing environmental consciousness and the mounting realization that human progress shouldn't come at the expense of the planet.

Spokane transformed itself for Expo '74, creating a unique blend of urban and natural spaces. The fairgrounds, now Riverfront Park, were designed to embody the theme of environmental conservation, showcasing a balance between urban growth and nature.

The Expo drew millions of visitors, elevating Spokane's stature and transforming it into a beacon for environmental sustainability. It set a new precedent for future World's

Expo '74 collage card

Fairs, highlighting the importance of environmental consciousness in city planning, architectural design, and technology development.

This fair was not just a celebration; it was a global call to action, an invitation to rethink our relationship with the environment. It underlined the growing awareness that the earth's resources are finite and the need to balance economic growth with environmental preservation.

India's 'Smiling Buddha': A Nuclear Power Rises - May 18th

India, the world's largest democracy, surprised the world with its first nuclear test. Code-named 'Smiling Buddha,' the test was an assertive step that catapulted India into the league of nuclear-armed nations.

Conducted at the Pokhran Test Range in the vast expanses of the Rajasthan desert, this underground explosion was seen as a technological triumph and a strategic imperative. The test was a clear message to the world and neighboring countries of India's technological prowess and its intent to safeguard its sovereignty.

The New York Times Archives

This action, though controversial, was seen within India as a necessary step for its national security, given its contentious relationships with its nuclear-armed neighbors, China and Pakistan. It also reflected India's ambitions of being a major player in the international arena. The 'Smiling Buddha' had significant global implications. It changed the dynamics of the South Asian region, marking the beginning of an arms race. It also spurred a worldwide debate about nuclear proliferation and arms control, culminating in the Nuclear Suppliers Group's formation to control nuclear technology transfer.

India's first successful nuclear weapon test demonstration

Nixon Resigns: Watergate's Shocking Climax - August 8th

The Morning News front page

In 1974, a political earthquake shook the United States to its core. President Richard Nixon, embroiled in the infamous Watergate scandal, chose resignation over impeachment, becoming the first U.S. President to resign from office.

The Watergate scandal, named after the Watergate complex, where the Democratic National Committee's headquarters was broken into, began with a seemingly inconsequential burglary. However, investigations by two relentless journalists, Bob Woodward and Carl Bernstein of The Washington Post, revealed it to be the tip of an iceberg of political espionage, cover-ups, and corruption that reached the highest levels of power. Nixon's resignation was more than just an individual's fall from grace; it was a critical moment in American history that undermined the nation's faith in the presidency and government. It highlighted the importance of a free press and the checks and balances in the American political system.

Other Major Events

China's Terracotta Army: A Spectacular Discovery - March 29th

The year 1974 witnessed one of the most significant archaeological discoveries of the 20th century: the Terracotta Army of China's first emperor, Qin Shi Huang. Unearthed near Xi'an in Shaanxi province, this vast array of life-sized terracotta soldiers, horses, and chariots provided an unparalleled glimpse into China's past. The Terracotta Army was not just a show of the emperor's might but also a representation of his beliefs

Terracotta Army

in life after death and his readiness for it. Each of the thousands of statues was distinct, indicating the remarkable level of craftsmanship and sophistication in ancient Chinese society.

Terracotta warrior in a museum

The discovery stirred global excitement, turning the world's spotlight on China's rich history. It underscored the cultural significance of archaeological research and preservation, illustrating the power of such discoveries in bridging the past and present.

This Terracotta Army, a standing testament to a civilization's grandeur from over two millennia ago, continues to captivate millions, bringing them closer to understanding the mystique that shrouds ancient China and its first emperor.

Tornado Terror: The US's Worst Outbreak - April 3rd-4th

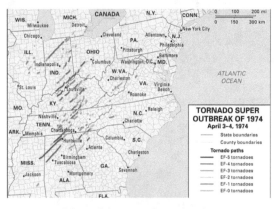

Map of the tornado outbreak

In the spring, an unprecedented weather event unfolded in the United States, a massive tornado outbreak stretching from the Great Lakes to the deep South. Known as the 'Super Outbreak,' it remains one of the most severe tornado episodes in recorded history.

The event consisted of a series of 148 tornadoes over thirteen states, inflicting significant loss of life and substantial property damage. The scale and impact of this weather event underscored the need for enhanced meteorological research, early warning systems, and public education about tornado preparedness and safety.

A trail of destruction

This event marked a turning point in the field of meteorology. It drove significant advancements in weather forecasting technology, including the development of Doppler radar, which allows meteorologists to detect weather patterns and storm rotation more accurately. It also spurred improvements in emergency management and disaster response, mitigating the potential impacts of future outbreaks.

Portugal's Revolution: Dictatorship Overthrown - April 25th

Soldiers and civilians celebrating with carnations

Portugal experienced a seismic political shift that would forever change the country's trajectory. After nearly half a century of autocratic rule under the 'Estado Novo' regime, the 'Carnation Revolution' peacefully overthrew the dictatorship, marking the dawn of a new democratic era.

Led by military officers who formed the Armed Forces Movement, the revolution, surprisingly non-violent, saw civilians join soldiers in the streets, offering them carnations that were famously placed in the barrels of their guns - hence the revolution's name.

The Carnation Revolution ended the longest dictatorship in Europe, paving the way for a democratic Portugal. It also marked the beginning of the end for Portugal's colonial empire, with independence soon granted to its African colonies.

The peaceful overthrow of the dictatorship was a critical moment for Portugal and the world, illustrating the power of non-violent resistance and the universal yearning for freedom and democracy.

A Global Health Leap: WHO's Immunization Expansion - May 23rd

In 1974, the World Health Organization (WHO) embarked on an ambitious global health initiative, the Expanded Programme on Immunization (EPI). This program aimed to provide universal immunization for all children against six major diseases: Tuberculosis, Polio, Diphtheria, Tetanus, Pertussis, and Measles.

EXPANDED PROGRAMME ON IMMUNIZATION 1974

World Health Organization

EPI logo

Before EPI, immunization coverage was staggeringly low in many parts of the world, particularly in low-income countries. Vaccines, despite being one of the most cost-effective health interventions, were not reaching many children, resulting in preventable illness and death.

EPI marked a significant step forward in global health. It represented a concerted effort to bridge the health equity gap and protect every child, no matter where they were born, from preventable diseases. The program galvanized international cooperation, garnering support from governments, non-governmental organizations, and the private sector.

Since its inception, EPI has led to a significant reduction in child mortality worldwide and the eradication of smallpox, one of humanity's most significant public health victories. The legacy of EPI continues to shape global health, underlying the principle that access to essential healthcare, including immunization, is a fundamental human right.

Ali vs Foreman: "The Rumble in the Jungle" - October 30th

On a steamy night in Kinshasa, Zaire (now the Democratic Republic of Congo), one of the most famous boxing matches of all time took place. The heavyweight title bout, fittingly

Two boxing giants

dubbed 'The Rumble in the Jungle,' saw the charismatic and skillful Muhammad Ali take on the fearsome George Foreman. The match was more than a boxing event; it was a global spectacle, a strategic chess game in the ring, and a clash

Muhammad Ali got the better of George Foreman in round eight

of personalities. Ali, the underdog, used a novel strategy, later known as the 'rope-a-dope,' enduring punches while leaning against the ropes, causing Foreman to exhaust himself.

Ali's triumph in the eighth round was not just a victory in the ring but a victory of intellect, courage, and resilience. It was a defining moment in his career that cemented his status as one of the greatest boxers of all time.

'The Rumble in the Jungle' transcended the world of boxing. It captured the world's imagination, bringing global attention to Africa. It was a testament to the universal appeal of sports and its power to unite people across borders and cultures.

Political Events

Solzhenitsyn: Banished by the Soviet Union - February 12th

In 1974, Soviet authorities forcibly expelled one of their most eminent writers, Aleksandr Solzhenitsyn, from his motherland. A decorated World War II veteran, Solzhenitsyn's writings on the brutal realities of the Soviet Gulag labor camps had earned him the ire of the state.

Solzhenitsyn's works were not just fictional narratives; they were powerful indictments of the Soviet regime's repressive practices, based on his own experiences as a prisoner. His writings were a clarion call for freedom, truth, and the inviolable dignity of the individual.

His banishment marked a low point in Soviet intellectual and cultural life, signaling the regime's unwillingness to tolerate dissent. However, it also amplified Solzhenitsyn's voice on the global stage, garnering international attention to human rights abuses in the Soviet Union.

Aleksandr Solzhenitsyn

Solzhenitsyn's exile and his courageous stand against tyranny emphasized the vital role of writers and intellectuals in safeguarding freedom and human rights. His works continue to resonate, serving as powerful reminders of the perils of unchecked power and the importance of free speech.

Perón: Argentina's Historic Female President - July 1st

Isabel Perón

In the wake of her husband Juan Perón's death, Isabel Perón, his third wife, ascended to Argentina's presidency, becoming the first woman to hold this office in the Western Hemisphere. Her ascension was a reflection of the popularity of the Peronist movement, an ideological blend of labor rights, social welfare, and political justice, encapsulated in Juan Perón's three-pillar mantra: "Justice, Community, and Independence."

Isabel Perón's presidency was loaded with

economic instability, social unrest, and increased violence by leftist guerrillas and right-wing paramilitary forces. Her administration faced criticism for its handling of the economy and allegations of corruption.

Despite the controversy surrounding her presidency, Isabel Perón's rise to power was emblematic of the political turbulence characterizing Argentina in the 1970s. It also marked an important milestone in the struggle for gender equality in political representation, serving as an inspiration for future female leaders.

Ford's Presidency: A New Dawn for America - August 9th

In the aftermath of Richard Nixon's shocking resignation amid the Watergate scandal, Vice President Gerald Ford assumed the presidency, ushering in a new era in American politics.

Ford's ascension to the presidency marked a critical juncture in American history. Faced with the monumental task of restoring public trust in the presidency, Ford's administration was defined by its efforts to heal the nation's wounds and move beyond the Watergate scandal.

Gerald Ford

Ford's presidency, while brief, was marked by significant developments. He grappled with inflation, energy crises, and continued Cold War tensions. His controversial decision to pardon Nixon was seen by many as a necessary step to put the Watergate scandal to rest and focus on the nation's pressing issues.

Gerald Ford's presidency symbolized a period of transition and healing for the United States. It highlighted the resilience of American democracy in the face of crisis and the importance of integrity and accountability in public office.

Kootenai vs US: War Declared - September 20th

In 1974, a small Native American tribe, the Kootenai, did something unthinkable: they declared war against the United States. No blood was spilled, no bullets fired. It was a symbolic war, a desperate call for attention to their predicament and a demand for their rightful land. The Kootenai's declaration of war highlighted the long-standing grievances of Native American tribes against the U.S. government over land rights and broken treaties. It drew national attention to the tribe's struggle for survival and its quest to reclaim its ancestral territory.

The declaration of war

The Kootenai's war culminated in the creation of a minuscule reservation, a compromise that fell short of the tribe's demands but nonetheless represented a small victory. It marked an important moment in Native American activism and the broader fight for indigenous rights in the United States.

Other Notable Events

Preserving Fuel: US Imposes 55 MPH Limit - January 2nd

In response to the 1973 oil crisis sparked by the OPEC embargo, the United States took an extraordinary measure to conserve fuel. A nationwide speed limit of 55 miles per hour was imposed under the Emergency Highway

55 MPH speed limit in Route 61

Energy Conservation Act. This move illustrated the profound impact of the oil crisis on everyday life in America and the world. It reflected the increasing awareness of energy as a finite resource and the need for conservation.

The speed limit, though unpopular and often disregarded, led to reductions in fuel consumption and, unexpectedly, a decrease in highway fatalities. This legislation highlighted the interplay between energy policy, environmental considerations, and public safety.

'Blazing Saddles': Brooks' Wild West Hits Big Screen - February 7th

In 1974, audiences were treated to an audacious comedy that left no sacred cows untouched: Mel Brooks' 'Blazing Saddles.' The film brilliantly satirized the Western genre, exploring themes of racism and power structures through its irreverent humor.

'Blazing Saddles' wasn't just a comedic romp; it was a potent social commentary. Using its Western setting as a canvas, the film critiqued contemporary societal issues, with Brooks' distinctive brand of humor challenging audience expectations and stereotypes.

Despite its initial controversy, 'Blazing Saddles' became a cultural phenomenon,

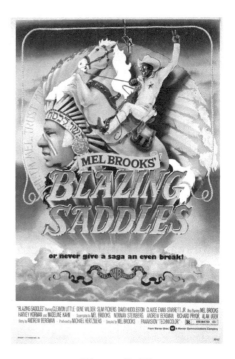

Blazing Saddles

demonstrating the power of comedy as a tool for social commentary. It has since been praised for its daring humor and incisive critique of racism, establishing its place in cinematic history.

Hiroo Onoda walks from the jungle

Final Surrender: Last Japanese Soldier Bows Out - March 11th

In a tale as fascinating as it was unusual, Hiroo Onoda, a former Japanese army intelligence officer, emerged from his hideout in the Philippine jungle, finally surrendering, a full 29 years after World War II had ended.

Onoda's story is a poignant testament to the lasting impact of war on individuals and societies.

Unaware that the war had ended, he remained loyal to his orders, surviving in the wilderness and awaiting a command to stand down that had technically come decades earlier.

His return to Japan was met with astonishment and admiration, and his tale gripped the world, stressing the potent combination of military indoctrination, personal resilience, and the human will to survive.

He salutes after handing over a military sword

Greece's Fresh Start: Military Regime Ends - July 24th

After seven years of military rule marked by repression and human rights abuses, Greece emerged from the shadow of dictatorship. The regime's collapse paved the way for the restoration of democracy, marking a turning point in modern Greek history.

Tanks surrounded the Greek parliament

The fall of the dictatorship was precipitated by its mishandling of the Cyprus crisis, which resulted in a military invasion by Turkey and a consequential political fiasco. The public's mounting disillusionment and domestic and international pressure culminated in a peaceful transition back to civilian rule.

The end of the military regime signified a rebirth for Greece, marking the beginning of the 'Metapolitefsi' period characterized by political stability and the consolidation of democracy.

'The Wiz' Musical Unveiled – October 21st

In October, Broadway was poised for a revolution. The curtain rose at the Morris A. Mechanic Theatre in Baltimore, unveiling "The Wiz: The Super Soul Musical 'Wonderful Wizard of Oz'." This innovative work, brought to life by composer Charlie Smalls and writer William F. Brown, offered a brilliant retelling of L. Frank Baum's 1900 classic 'The Wonderful Wizard of Oz,' but with a twist. Set against the backdrop of contemporary African American culture, it breathed fresh life into an age-old tale.

The show's monumental impact was evident when it transitioned to Broadway's esteemed Majestic Theatre on January 5th, 1975, with a renewed cast. The 1975 Broadway iteration clinched seven Tony Awards, including the coveted Best Musical, signifying Broadway's emerging embrace of productions with all-Black casts.

Tracks like "Ease on Down the Road" became instant classics, while the narrative's reimagined context of identity and belonging resonated

The Wiz poster

profoundly. The musical's cultural significance wasn't limited to the stage. In 1978, a grand film adaptation hit the screens, with notable names like Ted Ross and Mabel King revisiting their iconic roles. Later, the world witnessed a live television adaptation, 'The Wiz Live!', aired on NBC in 2015, paying homage to this timeless masterpiece.

As the lights dimmed and applause echoed, it became clear: 'The Wiz' wasn't merely a musical. It was, and remains, an emblem of change, representing the power of reimagined classics through diverse cultural lenses.

The show on stage

Chapter II: Crime & Punishment 1974

Major Crime Events

Theodore Bundy

Bundy's Reign of Terror Begins – January 4th

The dawn of 1974 unveiled the malevolence of Ted Bundy, an infamous serial killer whose charm masked his sadistic intent. This handsome figure, once an active member of a Seattle suicide hotline, was an anomaly, shattering conventional images of criminals. Juggling a facade of a dedicated law student, Bundy's darker side lurked beneath, unleashing a terror that gripped the nation.

His first acts of horror emerged in the Pacific Northwest, where young women, mainly college students, inexplicably vanished. While he maintained his innocence using cunning and charm, often feigning injuries to prey on empathy or impersonating authority, his modus operandi was consistent: lure, incapacitate, sexually assault, and then murder. After a decade of denial, Bundy confessed to 30 murders from 1974 to 1978, though the real count remains ambiguous.

His prolonged evasion from capture exposed gaps in police cooperation and data sharing. Consequently, this led to the evolution of law enforcement methods, including refined communication among agencies and the heightened use of forensic science – a somber testament to this gruesome chapter in crime history.

Patty Hearst: Kidnapped, Brainwashed, Unforgettable - February 4th

Patty Hearst

When newspaper heiress Patty Hearst was kidnapped by the Symbionese Liberation Army (SLA), an urban guerrilla group, the United States was plunged into one of the most bizarre sagas of its history. The SLA, utilizing the Hearst abduction as a tool to gain national attention for their radical political ideas, sent shockwaves through the American public.

But the narrative took an unforeseen twist. Hearst, seemingly brainwashed by her captors, took part in a bank robbery alongside the SLA members. The transformation of the heiress into a gun-toting revolutionary posed unprecedented legal, ethical, and psychological questions about identity, free will, and the effects of coercive persuasion. The resultant trial was a media sensation, with Hearst's defense centered on the argument of brainwashing and coercion. The implications of the Hearst case extended far beyond its media and legal spectacle. The event spurred research into the field of psychological manipulation, particularly Stockholm Syndrome, leading to new understandings of victim and captor dynamics.

A Royal Scare: Princess Anne's Kidnap Attempt - March 20th

March marked a disturbing chapter in Britain's royal history when Princess Anne narrowly escaped an audacious kidnap attempt. A mentally disturbed man named Ian Ball planned to secure a hefty ransom from the Queen. This shocking event played

Princess Anne

out on a public street, as the princess was returning to Buckingham Palace from a charity event.

Despite the grave danger, Princess Anne displayed remarkable courage and presence of mind. With her skillful handling of the situation and the timely intervention of her protection officer and a few brave passersby, a potentially disastrous event was averted.

The aftermath of the incident led to a thorough revision of the royal security measures, sparking debate about the delicate balance between public accessibility to royal figures and their personal safety. The event also emphasized the challenges faced by law enforcement in predicting and preventing the actions of lone-wolf attackers, leading to significant changes in security protocols.

It made the headlines

Park Chung-Hee

Presidential Peril: Failed Hit on Park Chung-hee - August 15th

South Korean history witnessed a shocking episode when President Park Chung-hee, a polarizing figure, was the target of an assassination attempt. The event, orchestrated by a North Korean sympathizer, tragically culminated in the death of First Lady Yuk Young-soo, casting the nation into mourning.

Park Chung-hee's presidency, characterized by both rapid economic development and severe political repression, has long been the subject of intense debate. The failed assassination attempt only added to the complexity of his legacy.

Yuk Young-soo, embraces a baby in an orphanage near Bonn, Germany in 1964

Park's stern response to the attempt, characterized by further clamping down on internal dissidents and adopting a hardened stance towards North Korea, exacerbated the existing political and societal tensions. The event played a crucial role in shaping South Korea's political trajectory, emphasizing the delicate balance between national security and democratic values.

Chapter III: Entertainment 1974

Silver Screen

Top Film of 1974: Blazing Saddles

"Blazing Saddles", a western satire co-written and directed by Mel Brooks, was released in 1974. The movie features a black sheriff, played by Cleavon Little, in a racist town, and a washed-up gunslinger, played by Gene Wilder. The plot explores the reactions of the townsfolk and the attempts of a corrupt state attorney general to drive the sheriff out of town. The film originally developed from Andrew Bergman's story outline called Tex-X. Despite a chaotic writing process and almost being unreleased, the film became a

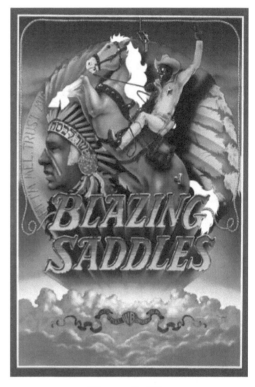

Blazing Saddles

hit, even leading to a successful reissue in 1976 and 1979.

The film's gross revenue totaled $119.5 million from rentals in the US and Canada, making it one of the few films at the time to cross the $100 million mark. Critical reception was mixed upon release, with some praising its boldness and humor, while others criticized its chaotic structure and stale jokes. Today, it is recognized as a classic, known for its daring, provocative, and humorous take on racial prejudice.

The film received three nominations at the 47th Academy Awards, including Best Supporting Actress for Madeline Kahn. In 2006, it was selected for preservation in the National Film Registry by the Library of Congress for its cultural, historical, and aesthetic significance. It's still considered a biting satire on racism, although its treatment of women and the gay community is seen as less progressive.

Remaining Top 3

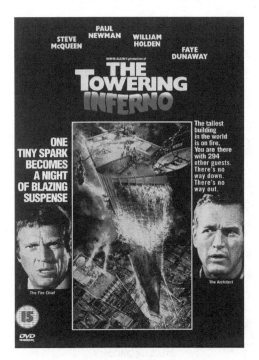

The Towering Inferno

The Towering Inferno

"The Towering Inferno" is a disaster film produced by Irwin Allen and directed by John Guillermin. This movie, a unique collaboration between Warner Bros. and 20th Century Fox, was adapted from the novels "The Tower" by Richard Martin Stern and "The Glass Inferno" by Thomas N. Scortia and Frank M. Robinson. This joint venture ensured that two competing films about a similar disaster didn't end up cannibalizing each other's audiences. The story revolves around a catastrophic fire in the world's tallest building, The Glass Tower, due to compromised electrical wiring, leading to frantic rescue operations. It was theatrically released on December 16th, 1974, to critical acclaim. Lead actors Steve McQueen and Paul Newman, who were paid a then-unprecedented $1 million each, delivered particularly praiseworthy performances. Despite its extensive runtime, the film's enthralling plot and impressive visual effects have etched it as a classic in the disaster genre. Garnering eight Academy Award nominations and winning three, it continues to be a significant marker in Hollywood cinema history.

The Trial of Billy Jack

The Trial of Billy Jack

"The Trial of Billy Jack" is a 1974 Western action film, the sequel to the 1971 film "Billy Jack". The film revolves around the titular character facing an involuntary manslaughter charge, the rebuilding efforts of an experimental school for troubled youth, and the escalating tensions between the school and local town. Despite its commercial success, grossing $9 million in its opening five days, the film was widely panned by critics, with Vincent Canby of The New York Times describing it as "three hours of naiveté". Critics also criticized its 170-minute running time and felt it lacked focus. An accompanying newspaper ad campaign for the film's 1975 reissue attacked critics for being out of touch with mass audiences. Despite its initial success, this film marked the effective end of the Billy Jack series, with subsequent films not seeing widespread theatrical release or completion. The film was directed by Tom Laughlin and also starred Delores Taylor.

 Top 1974 Movies at The Domestic Box Office (the-numbers.com)

Rank	Title	Date	Total Gross
1	Blazing Saddles	Feb 7, 1974	$119,500,000
2	Towering Inferno	Dec 16, 1974	$116,000,000
3	The Trial of Billy Jack	Jan 1, 1974	$89,000,000
4	Young Frankenstein	Dec 15, 1974	$86,300,000

Rank	Title	Date	Total Gross
5	Earthquake	Nov 15, 1974	$79,700,000
6	The Godfather: Part II	Dec 11, 1974	$57,300,000
7	Airport 1975	Oct 18, 1974	$47,285,152
8	The Life and Times of Grizz…	Nov 13, 1974	$45,411,063
9	The Longest Yard	Aug 30, 1974	$43,008,075
10	Murder on the Orient Express	Nov 22, 1974	$35,733,867

Other Film Releases

From the gritty streets of Los Angeles to the dystopian future, 1974 was a remarkable year in cinema. A diverse range of film styles and stories graced the silver screen, carving a unique niche in the archives of film history. While the box-office blockbusters grabbed the limelight, a few underdogs slipped under the radar, only to reemerge as cult favorites in the years that followed. Among them were six extraordinary films: "Chinatown", "The Texas Chain Saw Massacre", "Phantom of the Paradise", "Dark Star", "Female Trouble", and "Zardoz."

"Chinatown", directed by the talented Roman Polanski and featuring Jack Nicholson at his finest, was a neo-noir mystery that painted a portrait of

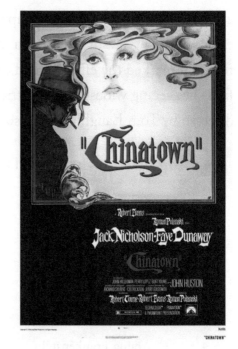

Chinatown

corruption and intrigue in 1930s Los Angeles. Despite its initial success and critical acclaim, its lasting impact on film noir and the mystery genre renders it a cult classic.

"The Texas Chain Saw Massacre", meanwhile, sent shivers down the audience's spine, shaking the very foundation of the horror genre. Directed by Tobe Hooper, this terrifying tale of a group of friends falling prey to a family of cannibals in rural Texas has since been hailed as one of the most influential horror films ever made.

"Phantom of the Paradise", Brian De Palma's rock musical horror comedy, combined sharp satire with catchy tunes. Though it failed to resonate with the audience initially, its distinctive style and innovative storytelling have earned it a cult following over the years.

The Texas Chain Saw Massacre   Phantom of the Paradise

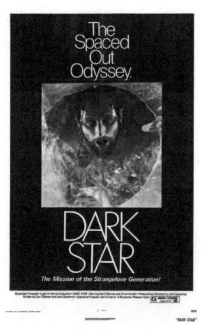

Dark Star

The outer space horror film "Dark Star", director John Carpenter's debut, did not make much noise at the box office initially. However, its existential dread, dark humor, and unique premise have since been recognized and celebrated in the sci-fi community.

In a similar vein, John Waters' "Female Trouble", a dark comedy brimming with his trademark transgressive humor, charts the life of a schoolgirl-turned-criminal in an outrageous narrative. The film's fearless exploration of taboos and subversion of societal norms have cemented its status as a cult favorite.

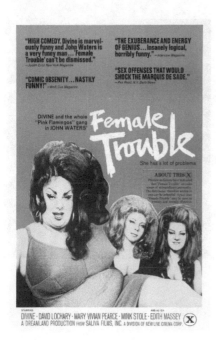

Female Trouble

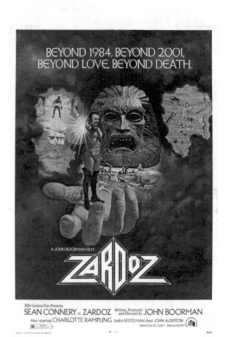

Zardoz

Lastly, "Zardoz", a visionary sci-fi film by John Boorman, depicted a post-apocalyptic world marked by stark class divisions and existential questions. Despite being initially dismissed as confusing and over-ambitious, its bold themes and striking visuals have fascinated a dedicated fan base, transforming it into a cult classic.

Each of these six films, in their own distinct ways, pushed boundaries, defied conventions, and offered something refreshingly different. While they may not have been commercial hits, their boldness, originality, and the enduring love of dedicated fans have firmly etched them into the pantheon of 1974's cult classics.

The 31st Golden Globe Awards – Saturday, January 26th, 1974

🏆 Winners

Best Motion Picture – Drama:
The Exorcist

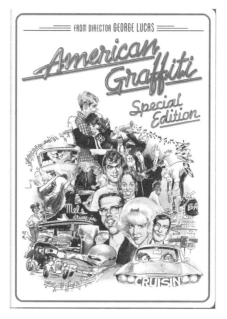

Best Motion Picture - Comedy or Musical: American Graffiti

Best Performance in a Motion Picture –
Drama – Actor: Al Pacino (Serpico)

Best Performance in a Motion Picture –
Drama – Actress:
Marsha Mason (Cinderella Liberty)

Best Performance in a Motion Picture
– Comedy or Musical – Actor:
George Segal (A Touch of Class)

Best Performance in a Motion Picture –
Comedy or Musical – Actress:
Glenda Jackson (A Touch of Class)

Best Supporting Performance in a Motion
Picture – Drama, Comedy or Musical –
Actor: John Houseman (The Paper Chase)

Best Supporting Performance in a Motion
Picture – Drama, Comedy or Musical –
Actress: Linda Blair (The Exorcist)

Best Director:
William Friedkin (The Exorcist)

Best Screenplay:
William Peter Blatty (The Exorcist)

The 27th British Academy Film Awards – 1974

⬥ Winners

Best Film:
Day for Night (François Truffaut)

Best Direction:
François Truffaut (Day for Night)

Best Actor:
Walter Matthau (Charley Varrick)

Best Actress:
Stéphane Audran (The Discreet Charm
of the Bourgeoisie)

Best Supporting Actor:
Arthur Lowe (O Lucky Man!)

Best Supporting Actress:
Valentina Cortese (Day for Night
as Severine)

Best Screenplay: Luis Buñuel and Jean-Claude
Carrière (The Discreet Charm of the Bourgeoisie)

The 46th Academy Awards – Tuesday, April 2nd, 1974 – Dorothy Chandler Pavilion, Los Angeles, California

Best Actor in a Leading Role:
Jack Lemmon (Save the Tiger)

Best Actress in a Leading Role:
Glenda Jackson (A Touch of Class)

Best Supporting Actor:
John Houseman (The Paper Chase)

Best Supporting Actress:
Tatum O'Neal (Paper Moon)

Best Director:
George Roy Hill (The Sting)

Best Music (Song):
Marvin Hamlisch (The Way We Were)

Best Cinematography:
Sven Nykvist (Cries and Whispers)

Best Film: The Sting

Top of the Charts

The 1970s were a vibrant, expansive, and eclectic era for music, bridging the countercultural spirit of the late 1960s and the flashy decadence of the early 1980s. As the dawn of a new decade set in, the 70s brought about a shift from the folksy, protest song era of the previous decade, towards a more diverse and extravagant soundscape. The rise of disco, with its flamboyant flair, paved the way for an era of glittery dance floors, while punk rock emerged as the rebellious voice of the youth. Progressive rock bands extended the boundaries of rock music into new territories. Meanwhile, the roots of hip hop began to form in the urban areas, particularly in New York City.

Top Album: "Band on the Run" by Paul McCartney and Wings

"Band on the Run", the third studio album by Paul McCartney and Wings, remains an iconic 1970s rock treasure. Released in December 1973, it reached its zenith in 1974, toppling charts worldwide. Despite the initial turmoil of recording in Lagos, Nigeria, which saw band members departing and McCartney and his wife Linda getting mugged, the album emerged as a triumph. It encompassed a broad array of musical styles, showcasing McCartney's eclectic talents. Songs like "Jet" and the title track, "Band on the Run", remain timeless classics. Remarkably,

Band on the Run

the entire album was performed almost exclusively by Paul, Linda, and Denny Laine, with McCartney playing drums, lead guitar, and piano. The album went on to win the 1975 Grammy for Best Pop Vocal Performance and has since been hailed as McCartney's best post-Beatles work.

Best Albums and Singles

In 1974, a cornucopia of musical styles reigned. Elton John's dynamic "Greatest Hits" and the daring "Caribou" demonstrated his virtuosity, while Eric Clapton's blues-infused "461 Ocean Boulevard" echoed with

Greatest Hits

Caribou

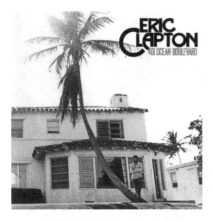

461 Ocean Boulevard

Court & Spark

introspective soundscapes. Joni Mitchell's "Court & Spark" contributed to the era's introspective bent, and David Bowie's "Diamond Dogs" added a touch of avant-garde rock. Meanwhile, Bad Company's self-titled album and Deep Purple's "Burn" continued to stoke the fires of hard rock.

Diamond Dogs

Burn

On the singles chart, Carl Douglas kicked it with "Kung Fu Fighting", Terry Jacks touched hearts with "Seasons in the Sun", and ABBA introduced themselves to the world with the unforgettable "Waterloo." With an eclectic mix of soulful ballads, hard rock, and catchy pop tunes, 1974 was a year when music truly rocked.

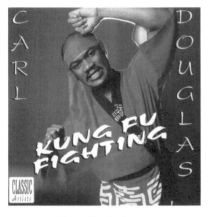

Kung Fu Fighting

Seasons in the Sun

Waterloo

♫ **Top Albums 1974 (tsort.info):**

1. Wings Band - On The Run
2. Elton John - Elton John's Greatest Hits
3. Eric Clapton - 461 Ocean Boulevard
4. Elton John - Caribou
5. Joni Mitchell - Court & Spark
6. David Bowie - Diamond Dogs
7. Marvin Hamlisch - The Sting
8. Bad Company - Bad Company
9. Deep Purple - Burn
10. Bachman-Turner Overdrive - Not Fragile

11. The Rolling Stones - It's Only Rock 'N' Roll

12. Bob Dylan - Planet Waves

🎵 Top Singles 1974 (tsort.info):

1. Carl Douglas - Kung Fu Fighting

2. Terry Jacks - Seasons in the Sun

3. George McCrae - Rock Your Baby

4. Abba - Waterloo

5. Bachman-Turner Overdrive - You Ain't Seen Nothin' Yet

6. Barbra Streisand - The Way We Were

7. Steve Miller Band - The Joker

8. The Hollies - The Air That I Breathe

9. Wings - Band On the Run

10. The Rubettes - Sugar Baby Love

11. Love Unlimited - Love's Theme

12. Paper Lace - The Night Chicago Died

The 16th Annual Grammy Awards – March 2nd, 1974 – Hollywood Palladium - Los Angeles, California

🏆 Winners

Record of the Year: Roberta Flack for
"Killing Me Softly With His Song"

Album of the Year:
"Innervisions" - Stevie Wonder

Song of the Year: "Killing Me Softly With His Song" - Charles Fox & Norman Gimbel (songwriters), performed by Roberta Flack

Best New Artist: Bette Midler

Television

In 1974, television was an evolving landscape, a far cry from the inundation of channels we see today. In the UK, viewers navigated between BBC1, BBC2, and ITV, with broadcasting hours limited, culminating with 'God Save The Queen'. Across the pond, America was an expanding TV universe, though ABC, CBS, and NBC reigned supreme. The year was a watershed moment in television history, introducing groundbreaking shows and sensational events that not only entertained millions but also sparked discussions and shifted cultural paradigms, leaving an indelible mark on the medium.

Happy Days

"Happy Days" Are Here: A 50s Nostalgia Ride Begins - January 15th

With the launch of "Happy Days", ABC ushered in a series that would transform television's portrayal of the past. It was a touchstone for those seeking the warmth of nostalgia, whisking viewers back to a simpler time. The show created an entire universe steeped in 50s culture, and Arthur "Fonzie" Fonzarelli, with his slicked-back hair and irresistible charm, quickly became a cultural phenomenon, symbolizing the timeless allure of cool.

Bagpuss

"Bagpuss" Arrives: An Icon of Children's Television is Born - February 2nd

As "Bagpuss" graced the screen for the first time on BBC2, a new icon of children's television was born. The saggy old cloth cat and his collection of lovable companions filled living rooms with enchantment, as viewers tuned in each week for tales infused with magic and warmth. The show's enduring popularity underscores the timeless quality of Firmin and Postgate's creation, its distinct charm capturing the hearts of generations.

"Good Times" Begins: Breaking Ground with African American Family Representation - February 8th

The premiere of "Good Times" marked a watershed moment in television. Its authentic portrayal of an African American family was a rarity in a landscape that often lacked diversity. The series offered a nuanced exploration of the Evans family's experiences, presenting comedic elements without downplaying the reality of their struggles. It broke ground, contributing significantly to the gradual shift towards more inclusive representation on television.

Archie Bunker's Stand: "All in the Family" Tackles Inflation - March 26th

"All in the Family" continued to break barriers with the powerful airing of "The Bunkers and Inflation: Part 4". Our everyday man, Archie Bunker, joining a protest after losing his job poignantly highlighted the economic turmoil of the era. It underscored the series' unwavering commitment to engage with contentious issues, pushing boundaries and setting a precedent for television's approach to social and political commentary, unrivaled for its time.

All in the Family

Homage to Frontier Life: "Little House on the Prairie" Premieres - March 30th

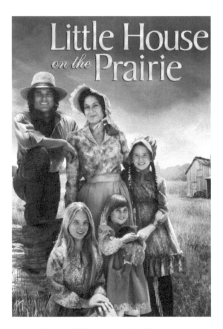

Little House on the Prairie

"Little House on the Prairie" delivered an idyllic view of American frontier life, resonating deeply with viewers. Its captivating depiction of the Ingalls family's challenges and triumphs brought the simplicity and hardship of pioneer life to the forefront. Laura's stories, portrayed with warmth and sincerity, offered a glimpse of hope, family bonds, and the uncomplicated pleasures of a life lived in harmony with nature.

Farewell to the Absurd: "Monty Python's Flying Circus" Airs its Final Episode - December 5th

Monty Python's Flying Circus

As the closing credits rolled on the last episode of "Monty Python's Flying Circus", audiences bid farewell to a show that had broken all the rules. From the Ministry of Silly Walks to the Dead Parrot sketch, the Pythons had pushed the boundaries of comedy, fusing intellect with silliness and satire with the absurd. The show's end was not just the finale of a series; it marked the conclusion of a comedic revolution, leaving a legacy that continues to inspire comedians worldwide.

📺 Television Ratings 1974 (classic-tv.com)

1973-74 Shows

Rank	Show	Estimated Audience
1	All in the Family	20,654,400
2	The Waltons	18,602,200
3	Sanford and Son	18,205,000

Rank	Show	Estimated Audience
4	M*A*S*H	17,013,400
5	Hawaii Five-O	15,888,000
6	Maude	15,557,000
7	Kojak	15,424,600
8	The Sonny and Cher Comedy Hour	15,424,600
9	The Mary Tyler Moore Show	15,292,200
10	Cannon	15,292,200

1974-75 Shows

Rank	Show	Estimated Audience
1	All in the Family	20,687,000
2	Sanford and Son	20,276,000
3	Chico and The Man	19,522,500
4	The Jeffersons	18,906,000
5	M*A*S*H	18,769,000
6	Rhoda	18,015,500
7	Good Times	17,673,000
8	The Waltons	17,467,500
9	Maude	17,056,500
10	Hawaii Five-O	16,988,000

The 31st Golden Globe Awards – Saturday, January 26th, 1974.

Best Musical/Comedy Series: All in the Family

Best Drama Series: The Waltons

Best Actor Drama Series:
James Stewart (Hawkins)

Best Actress - Drama Series:
Lee Remick (The Blue Knight)

Best Actress Musical/Comedy Series: Cher
(The Sonny & Cher Comedy Hour)

Supporting Actor in a Series,
Miniseries or Television Film:
McLean Stevenson (M*A*S*H)

Best Supporting Actress in a Series,
Miniseries or Television Film:
Ellen Corby (The Waltons)

Chapter IV: Sports Review 1974

American Sports

Super Bowl Triumph: Dolphins Take the Title - January 13th

Fullback Larry Csonka, named the game's MVP

In the Super Bowl VIII, the Miami Dolphins sealed a victory against the Minnesota Vikings, scoring 24-7 and marking their second consecutive Super Bowl win, emulating the earlier success of the Green Bay Packers. Hosted at Rice Stadium in Houston, Texas, this was a deviation from the usual venue choices of Los Angeles, Miami, or New Orleans, due to the Astrodome's smaller seating capacity. Interestingly, this was the last Super Bowl to feature goal posts at the front of the end zone. The Dolphins, marking their third consecutive Super Bowl appearance, maintained a strong lead throughout the game, squashing Minnesota's attempts at a comeback. Larry Csonka, the Dolphins' fullback, stole the show by setting Super Bowl records with his 145 rushing yards and 33 carries, earning the honor of being the first running back to be named Super Bowl MVP.

Celtics Conquer NBA Championship - May 12th

The 1973-74 NBA season wrapped up with an electrifying clash, where the Boston Celtics bested the Milwaukee Bucks in a nail-biting 4-3 series to lift the NBA championship. The Milwaukee Bucks, resplendent with stars like Kareem Abdul-Jabbar and Oscar Robertson, had made a formidable return to the finals after a three-year absence. Yet, the Bucks' championship aspirations took a hit with Lucius Allen's untimely injury. Meanwhile, the Celtics, returning with a vengeance after a dashed title hope the previous season due to John Havlicek's injury, seized their opportunity. With a revitalized Havlicek, and stars like Dave Cowens, Paul Silas, and Jo Jo White in prime form, the Celtics stormed their way to the finals. They defeated the Buffalo Braves and

Dave Cowens, right, of Boston Celtics presses Kareem Abdul-Jabbar of the Milwaukee

then dethroned the defending champions, the New York Knicks, setting up the championship face-off. The Celtics triumphed over the Bucks in a thrilling seven-game series, marking their last road game 7 victory until 2022.

King's Court: Billie Jean's US Open Victory - September 8th

Billie Jean during the US Open finals

In the summer, iconic tennis player Billie Jean King, founder of World TeamTennis, was considering skipping the US Open due to fatigue from the inaugural season of WTT. Despite her exhaustion, she decided to participate, fueled by her patriotic spirit and fear of lingering regret. King, who was the second seed that year, sailed into the semi-finals where she faced Julie Heldman. Following a three-set triumph over Heldman, King advanced to the finals to take on the Australian sensation, Evonne Goolagong. The final was a seesaw match, packed with electric rallies, which King described as some of her most memorable. King was able to mount a comeback after losing the first set to Goolagong and won the match 3-6, 6-3, 7-5. Reflecting on the victory, she credited her resilience and strong match-playing skills, admitting she felt like a guardian angel had helped her win that final.

Third Time Lucky: Athletics' World Series Hat-trick - October 17th

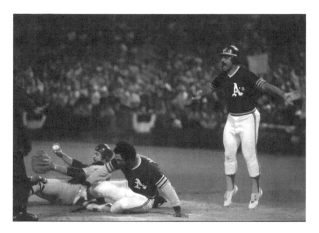

Reggie Jackson just beats Yeager's tag as Sal Bando jumps out of the way

In the historic 1974 World Series, the resilient Oakland Athletics clinched their third consecutive championship against the formidable Los Angeles Dodgers. A compelling series, the A's achieved a four-to-one victory after a split start in LA, asserting dominance in their three consecutive home games. Rollie Fingers shone brightly, contributing to three victories and receiving the World Series MVP Award. Meanwhile, the LA Dodgers, despite their impressive stats and a robust 102-game winning streak, stumbled at the crucial moment. The unique mix of athletic prowess and internal drama marked this World Series as a memorable event, with Oakland stamping their legacy as a 70s powerhouse. As the first all-California World Series, the Athletics-Dodgers clash foreshadowed future encounters, forever inscribing 1974 in the records of baseball history.

British Sports

Leeds United: Football League Champions - April 27th

Leeds United celebrating their victory

The 1973–74 season marked Leeds United's tenth consecutive First Division stint and saw them securing their second title. Manager Don Revie, dismissing a move to Everton, set an ambitious target of an unbeaten season.

Leeds ignited their campaign with seven straight league wins. A goalless draw with Manchester United ended their streak, but they remained focused on the league. Exits from the League and UEFA Cups didn't deter them. By the start of 1974, Leeds were eight points clear of second-placed Liverpool. Their first defeat to Stoke City did little to affect their momentum. Leeds finished the season with a then-record 29-game unbeaten run, unmatched until Arsenal's 2003–04 season. The season ended with Revie leaving to manage England.

Celtic FC: Scottish Football's Champions - May 6th

Celtic FC rocked the Scottish Premiership, storming to the title with some unforgettable moments of football magic. Under Neil Lennon, they became a team on fire, oozing skill, resilience, and

Celtic FC celebrating their title win

unmatched strategy. On the pitch, players like Callum McGregor, Odsonne Édouard, and James Forrest turned games on their heads, weaving magic with every touch. Their solid defense was the backbone of this successful campaign.

But this title run was more than just points and victories. It was about Celtic's spirit, their grit, and their thirst for excellence. This victory added another shiny trophy to their brimming cabinet, reaffirming their status as Scottish football giants. The 'Bhoys' had once again shown they were the kings of the Scottish game. They've painted the Premiership green and white, creating a season for the ages.

Golf Glory: Gary Player Takes British Open - July 13th

Gary Player holding his trophy at the 1974 British Open

The 103rd Open Championship of 1974, held at the distinguished Royal Lytham & St Annes Golf Club, was a notable event in golf's history. The stage was dominated by Gary Player, a South African golf maestro, who claimed his third Open Championship with a convincing four-stroke lead over Peter Oosterhuis. This significant victory marked Player's eighth major title, demonstrating his absolute dominance in the sport. 1974 was a stellar year for Player, who also claimed the Masters title and had top-ten finishes in both the U.S. Open and PGA Championship. This Open Championship solidified Player's status as one of golf's all-time greats and left an indelible mark on the sport's rich history.

Cricket Clash: England Bests India – July 17th

The Indian cricket team's tour of England in 1974 was marked by a series of defeats that labeled the season as the infamous "Summer of 42". This referred to India's dismal second innings score in the Second Test at Lord's. The disastrous tour culminated

Geoffrey Boycott, one of England's leading run-scorers

in England winning all five international matches.

At the peak of their game in the early 1970s, the Indian team had world-class spinners like Bhagwat Chandrasekhar, Bishen Singh Bedi, Erapalli Prasanna, and Srinivas Venkataraghavan. Sunil Gavaskar and Gundappa Vishwanath spearheaded the batting. However, their performances couldn't prevent a string of losses.

The First Test saw England triumph by 113 runs, while the Second Test concluded in a catastrophic defeat for India by an innings and 285 runs. The Third Test didn't turn out any better for India as England achieved victory by an innings and 78 runs. In the one-day internationals too, England held their ground, winning both matches. This tour marked a low point in Indian cricket history.

International Sports

Summit Triumph: First Women Conquer Manaslu Peak - May 4th

The majesty of Manaslu, standing as the eighth-highest mountain globally at 8,163 meters in the Nepalese Himalayas, saw a groundbreaking achievement. Under the leadership of Kyoko Sato, a brave all-female Japanese team took on the challenge, creating a remarkable chapter in mountaineering history. Their triumph secured their place in history as the first women to conquer a peak towering over 8,000 meters. The feat, an incredible display of courage and tenacity, shattered

Manaslu, Nepal, Himalaya

boundaries and became a beacon of inspiration for women climbers worldwide. However, this historic ascent came with a cost, as they mourned a team member's loss during the descent. Today, the story of these trailblazing women continues to inspire, as adventurers from across the globe come to experience the majesty and challenge of Manaslu, meaning "mountain of the spirit" in Sanskrit.

FIFA Frenzy: Germany World Cup Champions - July 7th

West Germany's Franz Beckenbauer became the first captain to lift the new FIFA trophy

The 1974 FIFA World Cup was the tenth edition of the global football tournament and was hosted by West Germany, including West Berlin, from June 13th to July 7th. The event saw the debut of the new FIFA World Cup Trophy, designed by Italian sculptor Silvio Gazzaniga, replacing the permanently retired Jules Rimet Trophy. This was the first World Cup to implement double rounds of group stages. The host nation, West Germany, conquered their second World Cup title, triumphing over the Netherlands with a 2-1 victory in the finals at the Olympiastadion in Munich. Notably, Australia, East Germany, Haiti, and Zaire made their inaugural appearances at the tournament's final stage. East Germany and Zaire's 1974 participation marked their only World Cup appearances, while East Germany's debut was also its last before the country's reunification in 1990.

USSR Basketball: World Champions Crowned - July 14th

The 7th FIBA World Championship held in Puerto Rico in 1974 saw the Soviet Union, led by Hall of Fame coach Vladimir Kondrashin, recapturing their global dominance in basketball. The pivotal match was a thrilling face-off with the USA, ending with

Quinn Buckner (No. 10) and Tom Boswell (No. 13) face Kresimir Cosic of Yugoslavia (No. 11)

a 105-94 victory for the Soviets. Their success was fueled by an outstanding performance by Alexander Salnikov who scored 38 points. Meanwhile, the tournament also marked the rise of Spain as a global challenger in basketball. With a team boasting multiple players who were integral to Real Madrid's continental power, including Wayne Brabender, Clifford Luyk, and Juan Antonio Corbalan, Spain finished fifth in the tournament. This signaled the beginning of Spain's later dominance in international basketball and marked a generation bridge between Spain's teams of the 1968 and 1980 Olympics. The championship concluded with the Soviet Union, Yugoslavia, and the United States sharing the podium, highlighting a riveting tournament.

Fittipaldi Fastest: Formula One Championship Winner - October 6th

(From left) Jody Scheckter, Niki Lauda, Emerson Fittipaldi and Clay Regazzoni were all major drivers involved in the battle to win the 1974 Formula One world championship

In the thrilling 28th season of the FIA Formula One, Emerson Fittipaldi, driving for McLaren, emerged as the star of the circuit. Following Jackie Stewart's retirement, the path to the championship was intense and fraught with competition. The defining moment came during the climactic United States Grand Prix. Fittipaldi and Clay Regazzoni entered the race neck-and-neck in the championship standings. However, as Regazzoni encountered handling problems, Fittipaldi seized the opportunity, securing a fourth-place finish. This result secured Fittipaldi's second World Championship, the first for McLaren and marked the onset of Marlboro's sponsorship success in Formula One. His victory came amid a season shadowed by the tragic losses of Peter Revson and Helmuth Koinigg, the latter at the US Grand Prix. The year 1974 also marked the establishment of permanent racing numbers, setting a new norm in the sport.

Chapter V: General 1974

Pop Culture

King of Horror: Stephen King's 'Carrie' Debuts - April 5th

Carrie (1974) dust jacket, first edition

In the quiet month of April, the world of horror was forever altered when a then unknown writer, Stephen King, released his debut novel, 'Carrie'. Narrating the eerie tale of a telekinetic high school girl, 'Carrie' was as spine-chilling as it was touching. With King's masterful ability to merge the ordinary with the nightmarish and delve deep into the human psyche's abyss, he promptly established himself as a pioneering force in the genre. This was only the beginning of a career that would terrify, captivate, and mesmerize millions for decades to come.

Home Run History: Hank Aaron Surpasses Babe Ruth - April 8th

Baseball history was made when Hank Aaron broke one of the sport's most revered records. With his 715th career home run, he surpassed the legendary

Hank Aaron

Babe Ruth. This moment, in front of a home crowd at Atlanta Stadium, was more than just a sporting milestone; it was a symbolic victory against racial prejudice, an assertion of black excellence in a game still grappling with the shadows of its segregated past.

Invention of the Rubik's Cube - Mid 1974 (Exact Date Unknown)

Sometime in the middle of the year, in the quiet corners of a Budapest design studio, a colorful, complex, and confounding creation was born. The brainchild of Hungarian architect Ernő Rubik, the Rubik's Cube quietly slipped onto the scene, too complex to be just a puzzle and too intriguing to be ignored. It was a marvel of mathematics and design, an object that challenged, fascinated, and bewildered. Though Rubik's Cube made its debut in

Rubik's cube

the mid-70s, it wasn't until the next decade, when it reached the shores of America, that it truly burst onto the pop culture scene. Imported by Ideal Toy Corp in 1980, the cube's popularity skyrocketed, captivating millions of kids and adults alike, each obsessively twisting and turning in a race against the clock to restore the cube's colored harmony.

Evel Knievel prepares for his Snake River Canyon jump in Idaho

Evel's Leap: Knievel's Failed Snake River Canyon Jump - September 8th

On a clear day in September, the world held its breath as Evel Knievel, the daredevil showman of the century, attempted his most audacious stunt yet: a leap across

Snake River Canyon in a steam-powered rocket. Though the jump ended in a dramatic failure, it only served to cement Knievel's legacy. In an era of slow-motion TV and larger-than-life personalities, his failure was as captivating as any of his many victories, a testament to his fearless spirit and flair for spectacle.

The Ramones

The Ramones: Punk's New Vanguard Plays First Gig - August 16th

August saw a seismic shift in the world of music when a little-known band from Queens, New York, called The Ramones, played their first gig. With their fast, aggressive sound, irreverent attitude, and stripped-back aesthetic, they offered a raw and electrifying alternative to mainstream rock. They sparked a punk revolution that would influence countless artists and resonate within the music industry for generations to come.

First UK McDonald's: A Fast-Food Invasion Begins - November 13th

November witnessed an American invasion of a different kind when McDonald's, the fast-food giant, opened its first restaurant in the UK.

The front counter and menu board of UK's first McDonald's

Situated in Woolwich, South-East London, this heralded a new era of dining. The Golden Arches promised speed, consistency, and affordability, turning meals into a quick, efficient affair. It marked the beginning of the fast-food revolution that would soon permeate British culture, altering the nation's culinary landscape forever.

 Most Popular Books from 1974 (goodreads.com)

- ✶ Where the Sidewalk Ends - Shel Silverstein

- ✶ Carrie - Stephen King

- ✶ Zen and the Art of Motorcycle Maintenance: An Inquiry Into Values (Phaedrus, #1) - Robert M. Pirsig

- ✶ Helter Skelter: The True Story of the Manson Murders - Vincent Bugliosi

- ✶ The Forever War (The Forever War, #1) - Joe Haldeman

- ✶ The Dispossessed: An Ambiguous Utopia - Ursula K. Le Guin

- ✶ Jaws (Jaws, #1) - Peter Benchley

- ✶ The Killer Angels (The Civil War Trilogy, #2) - Michael Shaara

- ✶ If Beale Street Could Talk - James Baldwin

- ✶ Alive: The Story of the Andes Survivors - Piers Paul Read

- ✶ The Mote in God's Eye (Moties, #1) - Larry Niven

- ✶ All the President's Men - Carl Bernstein

- ✶ All Things Bright and Beautiful (All Creatures Great and Small, #3-4) - James Herriot

- ✶ The Power Broker: Robert Moses and the Fall of New York - Robert A. Caro

Technological Advancements

84-Day Skylab Mission Culminates with Triumphant Earth Return – February 8th

Gerald P. Carr, Edward G. Gibson, and William R. Pogue (L-R) crewed Skylab 4

Skylab, the first American space station, marked a milestone in space exploration, serving as an orbital workshop, solar observatory, and Earth observation post. It hosted three astronaut crews, conducting hundreds of experiments over approximately 24 weeks. Skylab was a testament to human ingenuity, with the first crew undertaking extensive repairs, including the deployment of a parasol-like sunshade to control temperature. This helped prevent a potential disaster, such as overheating that could release poisonous gases. The last crew returned after an impressive 84-day tenure in space. Their prolonged stay highlighted human endurance in the harsh space environment and offered valuable insights into the physical and psychological effects of long-term space habitation.

Microprocessing Marvel: The Intel 8080 Arrives - April 1st

The Intel 8080 microprocessor dramatically reshaped the tech landscape and impacted everyday lives. Its groundbreaking design set the stage for a new generation of microcomputers like the MITS Altair 8800, which ran on the CP/M operating system, democratizing computer technology and leading to an era of unprecedented technological innovation.

Closed and open Intel 8080 processor

In addition to its industrial applications, the 8080 found its way into popular culture, powering the first commercially available arcade game, Gun Fight, and later, the iconic Space Invaders. Its influence is even reflected in Microsoft's foundational product, Microsoft BASIC, originally programmed for the 8080.

Not just a technological marvel of its time, the 8080 served as the precursor to the 8086 and later x86 processors, preserving core machine instructions and concepts that persist in modern computing. This chip, modest by today's standards, was a pioneer in its time, leaving a lasting legacy. Its enduring impact is evident in tributes like the asteroid 8080 Intel and phone numbers of tech companies like Microsoft and Intel, featuring "8080" in homage to this microprocessor.

The Heimlich Maneuver: A Lifesaving Innovation - June 1st

In the realm of medical advancements, Dr. Henry Heimlich introduced a novel technique to save choking victims – the Heimlich Maneuver. This procedure revolutionized the way

Dr. Henry Heimlich holding a copy of his memoir

we respond to choking incidents. The technique is ingeniously simple yet highly effective; it involves delivering a sharp upward thrust just below a person's ribcage, which forces an obstructing object out from the airway. Since its inception, the Heimlich Maneuver has been credited with saving innumerable lives, from everyday incidents in restaurants and homes to more dire emergencies.

Dr. Heimlich's procedure continues to be taught in first aid courses around the world, and its impact on emergency medicine cannot be overstated.

First UPC Barcode scanned

The UPC Era: Revolution in Product Identification - June 26th

The Universal Product Code (UPC), a barcode system used globally, made its debut in 1974 when a pack of Wrigley's gum was scanned in Ohio. Born from the inventive mind of Norman Joseph Woodland, the idea for the barcode system was inspired by Morse code, leading to a revolutionary two-dimensional version. UPCs, comprising 12 unique digits for each product, streamlined the shopping experience and invigorated retail supply chains worldwide. Woodland and his colleague Bernard Silver obtained a patent for their ingenious invention in 1952, forever changing the way we purchase items. These small barcodes that we see on everyday items have made an enormous impact on global trade, serving as a silent yet powerful driver of retail and economic growth.

Ozone Alert: CFC's Depletion Warning - June 28th

In environmental science, a significant and concerning discovery was made about the alarming rate of Earth's ozone layer depletion, attributed to chlorofluorocarbons, or CFCs. These chemicals, once abundantly used in aerosols, air conditioners, and refrigeration systems, were shockingly found to cause severe damage to the stratospheric ozone. This damage manifested in the form of the notorious "ozone hole."

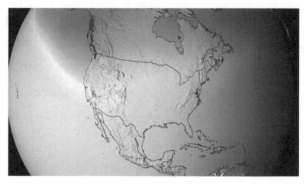

Computer predictions of what would have happened to the ozone layer in 1974 if CFCs had not been banned by the Montreal Protocol

The revelation of CFC's destructive effects sparked immediate international concern and action. It resulted in the landmark Montreal Protocol in 1987, a global agreement aiming to phase out CFC production and use, marking a milestone in international environmental cooperation.

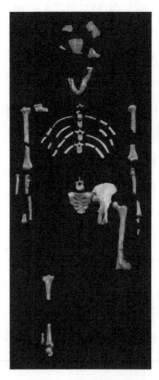

40% of Lucy's recovered skeleton

Unearthing 'Lucy': A Monumental Paleontological Find - November 24th

In the field of paleontology, a groundbreaking discovery was made when the fossilized remains of a hominid, affectionately named 'Lucy,' were unearthed in Ethiopia in 1974 by a team led by Donald Johanson. As an exemplar of the species Australopithecus afarensis, Lucy bridges the gap between apes and humans, providing invaluable insights into our own evolution. Her bipedalism – evidenced by her pelvic, femoral, and tibial structure – suggested that walking on two legs predated other human-like characteristics. This discovery reoriented and deepened our understanding of human ancestry, catalyzing a proliferation of new research avenues in human evolution.

Fashion

The 1970s was a colorful era of transformation for fashion, an evolution profoundly influenced by popular culture, shifting social norms, and the advent of new materials and styles. Both men's and women's fashion bore witness to dramatic shifts in style, each resonating with the spirit of the time.

Men's fashion began the journey with the slim-fitting pants of the mid-1960s and gradually progressed to the disco-infused wardrobe of low-rise bell bottoms and platform shoes.

Men's late 70s jeans

Turtlenecks were also a thing

Clothes took on a tighter fit, while fabrics such as polyester, velour, and terry cloth enjoyed newfound popularity. Leisure suits and tracksuits, popularized by John Travolta's "Saturday Night Fever" and associated with the athletic aesthetics of the '80s, became wardrobe staples. Hairstyles leaned towards longer locks, shirts remained untucked, and wide collars were in vogue, painting a picture of relaxed yet eclectic fashion sensibilities.

Elton John in a glam rock white suit

Davie Bowie in a stripy costume
designed by Kansai Yamamoto
for the Aladdin Sane tour

Glam rock, a cultural trend that soared in 1974, significantly impacted men's fashion. Icons like David Bowie and Elton John embodied this style, flamboyantly flaunting extravagant outfits and make-up, exhibiting an androgynous charm that redefined societal norms.

Simultaneously, women's fashion was a fascinating cocktail of the traditional and the experimental. The initial part of the decade saw a carryover of the "hippie" fashion from the late '60s, featuring floral patterns and flowing dresses with an array of different hemlines. The rise of palazzo pants simulated the look of a long skirt or dress, a style that was eventually replaced with the iconic wrap dress by Diane Von Furstenberg, praised for its flattering fit and adaptability.

70s Clothing Trends

As the decade matured, fashion took a bolder turn with the introduction of low-cut and bare-backed dresses. Ethnic prints and earthy tones painted the canvas of fashion, interspersed with pastel shades.

70s Clothing Trends

Diane von Furstenberg wearing wrap dress

Palazzo pants and long skirts

70s Summer Fashion

There was a conspicuous shift towards trousers over dresses, echoing the increasing participation of women in the workforce. The variety in skirt lengths added to the rich ensemble, giving women an array of choices to complement their blouses or shirts.

The 1970s was the decade of the boot, sported by both men and women. The allure of boots was driven by the variety of designs, from the crinkled texture to the exaggerated soles of the platform boots and the vintage charm of the "granny" boots. By the decade's end, however, fashion circled back to the conservative, with brown leather boots with short heels gaining popularity.

70s Dingo Boots for Men Ad

70s Boots for Women Ad

70s Boots for Women Ad

In essence, the 1970s represented an eclectic fusion of fashion, a testament to the decade's freedom of expression and the break from societal norms. From the vibrant glam rock look to the power statement of the wrap dress, the '70s left an enduring legacy in the history of fashion, continuing to inspire and shape the world of style to this day.

Cars

The car industry in 1974 was severely hit by the Middle East oil embargo, which led to skyrocketing fuel prices and dampened consumer confidence, resulting in significant layoffs and plant closures. U.S. auto production plummeted by 24% compared to the previous year. Volkswagen, the leading import, wasn't spared either. While the industry initially anticipated a surge in demand for compact and subcompact cars due to the fuel shortage, the latter half of the year saw an unexpected rebound in the sales of standard and luxury models, confounding automakers' predictions.

Top Selling Cars

U.S.A

Ford Pinto

As the top-selling car of 1974, the Ford Pinto proved to be a symbol of its era. With an impressive 360,688 units sold, it was a tangible response to the rising fuel costs and stringent federal regulations of the period. As a testament to its popularity, the Pinto's design even spawned a sibling in the form of the Mercury Bobcat, which was sold exclusively in Canada. Despite the economic turbulence of the time, the Pinto's cost-effectiveness and reliability made it a firm favorite among American consumers.

Plymouth Valiant

Just trailing the Pinto, the Plymouth Valiant made its mark with robust sales of 337,585 units. 1974 was a transformative year for the Valiant. Its frame was reshaped into a size similar to the Dart, with thicker C-pillars and new rear fender contours, all while retaining its distinctive 1973 front design elements. The introduction of the federal bumper standards further added to its heft. The Valiant's range broadened in 1974 with the inclusion of the luxurious "Scamp package" and the Brougham trim.

U. K.

The Ford Cortina held the crown as the best-selling car in the UK in the mid-70s, navigating through a significant recession. In 1974, the Cortina sold a remarkable 131,243 units, capturing a substantial 10.3% market share. Despite facing economic turmoil,

1974 Ford Cortina

sales in 1975 remained robust at 106,787 units. The Cortina's blend of comfort, style, and reliability struck a chord with UK buyers, securing its place at the top of the sales charts during this period.

In a close second, the Ford Escort displayed impressive performance in the UK market. In 1974, the Escort registered 91,699 sales, accounting for a 7.2% market share. The following year, the

1974 Ford Escort

Escort edged closer to its sibling, the Cortina, with sales increasing to 103,817 units. The Escort, a small family car, experienced notable success in Britain. It boasted six generations between 1968 and 2000, often dominating sales charts in the 80s and 90s. Its enduring popularity and continued evolution underline the Escort's significant role in Ford's UK market history.

Fastest Car

Lamborghini Countach LP400

In 1974, the Lamborghini Countach LP400, a vision of polygonal dynamism, redefined the supercar landscape. Boasting an unrivalled top speed of 179 mph (288 km/h), this mid-engine beast was powered by a 3.9-liter V-12 engine that churned out 370 horsepower. The Countach, birthed from a feud between automotive titans Enzo Ferrari and Ferruccio Lamborghini, kickstarted the era of wedge-shaped supercars. Not just a speed demon, the Countach was also a design icon, most notably in its Argento silver finish with a tobacco brown interior.

In short, it not only led the year in speed but also set a new standard for supercar aesthetics.

Most Expensive American Car of 1974

The most expensive American car of 1974 was the Lincoln Continental Mark IV, priced at $10,194. Manufactured by Ford from 1972 to 1976, it was marketed as a personal luxury car, with little direct competition. The Mark IV shared its chassis with the

1974 Lincoln Mark IV

Ford Thunderbird and included exclusive features such as a radiator-style grille, hidden headlights, and a Continental spare tire trunk lid. In 1976, a Designer Series option was introduced, offering specially coordinated exterior and interior trims.

A significant redesign in 1973 introduced 5 mph bumpers and a standard vinyl roof from 1973 onwards.

Most Powerful Muscle Car of 1974

1974 Pontiac SD-455 Trans Am

The Pontiac SD-455 Trans Am, the last muscle car of its era, was the most powerful of all 1974 muscle cars. Amidst rising emissions standards and insurance regulations, the Super Duty 455 was launched in 1972 and was initially said to output 310 horsepower. However, after environmental regulations, the horsepower fell to 290. Despite this, it garnered positive reception from enthusiasts. In 1973, only 295 Super Duty models were made, and 1,001 were produced in 1974. Other Firebird variations included the Formula 350, 400, and 455, and the compact Ventura GTO option.

Popular Recreation

As the peace and love momentum of the 1960s slowly faded into the background, the 1970s swung into gear with a burst of energy all its own. The era was a mix of contradictions, blending into an eclectic mix of disco dancing and Dungeons & Dragons.

Dancing at Ann Arbor's Newest Disco

It was a decade marked by the quest for individuality yet also fostered a collective culture of popular leisure activities that united communities, both physically and virtually.

Dancing in a disco, Mecklenburg, East Germany, 1974

In 1974, as disco beats pulsated through colorful dance floors, people found escape from their routines. The exhilarating dance style invited all, regardless of age or skill level, to groove to the rhythm. It wasn't just about the dance, but also about the sense of unity it brought along. As people swayed to the Bee Gees' tunes under shimmering disco balls, they felt connected, forgetting their differences and immersing themselves in the joy of the moment.

A first printing of the original woodgrain box edition of Dungeons and Dragons

Simultaneously, the advent of a captivating game named "Dungeons & Dragons" was adding a novel twist to indoor recreation. This imaginative game redefined boundaries, taking players on thrilling fantasy quests without leaving their living rooms. Whether it was to navigate through treacherous dungeons or combat mythical creatures, this innovative role-playing game captured the hearts and minds of millions. The game proved so engrossing that people frequently spent hours exploring enchanted realms and embracing their alter egos as wizards, warriors, or rogues.

1974 also witnessed the collective societal ritual of gathering around the television for a good laugh. The sitcom "All in the Family" was a cultural phenomenon. Despite its comedic overtones, the show was renowned for addressing serious, controversial issues - from racism to women's liberation - in a palatable manner, sparking critical conversations in households across the country. Archie Bunker, the show's protagonist, became a household name, and his armchair in the Smithsonian National Museum of American History remains a testament to the series' impact.

Meanwhile, in the United Kingdom, strategic minds were battling over the board game "Risk." This game of diplomacy, conflict, and conquest became the nation's favorite toy in 1974.

Risk Board Game, 1974 edition

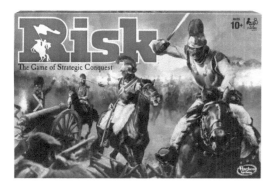

2016 edition

Family and friends would spend hours, or even days, trying to dominate the world, one territory at a time. The thrill of forming and dissolving alliances added a fascinating dimension to the game, making every round an unpredictable adventure.

Simultaneously, the game "Connect Four" was sweeping across living rooms and playgrounds alike. This simple yet engaging game proved that joy could be found in straightforward acts of connection, whether horizontal, vertical, or diagonal. "Connect Four" offered a break from the complex world, a small oasis of simplicity and fun that could be shared with anyone.

Of course, the 1970s were not just about disco dancing and board games. The decade also

Connect Four 1974 Edition, by Milton Bradley Company

1974 Mego Star Trek Carded Action Figure
- Capt. Kirk

saw a resurgence in bike riding, motivated by a heightened environmental consciousness. Star Trek fandom was on the rise, and collecting memorabilia became a cherished hobby. Photography, thanks to advancements in camera technology, was no longer a pursuit of the elite, but a widespread passion. Drive-in movies were the perfect spot for a family outing or a romantic date.

Customers at the Westbury Drive-In Theatre in Westbury, New York, attend an "Ape-a-Thon," which featured five of the Planet of the Apes movies

And pinball machines - those dazzling, clattering towers of light and sound - held pride of place in arcades, drawing crowds and stimulating fierce competition for the highest score.

Vintage Pinball Machine

In retrospect, 1974, like the rest of the 1970s, was a vibrant blend of cultural shifts and entertainment trends. As the disco ball turned, casting its multicolored glow over the dance floor, and as the dice rolled, deciding the fate of imaginary realms or world dominance, society was moving and evolving. It was a decade of change and growth, with popular recreational activities reflecting the spirit of the time - a spirit of fun, exploration, and connection that lives on in the cherished memories of those who were there.

Chapter VI: Births & Deaths 1974

Births (onthisday.com)

January 12th – Melanie C: English Singer-songwriter, DJ, Businesswoman and Media Personality

January 16th – Kate Moss: British Model and Fashion Designer

January 30th – Christian Bale: English Actor

January 30th – Olivia Colman: English Actress

February 7th – Steve Nash: Canadian Professional Basketball Coach and Former Player

February 8th – Seth Green: American Actor

February 10th – Elizabeth Banks: American Actress and Filmmaker

February 11th – Alex Jones: American Radio Host and Conspiracy Theorist

February 13th – Robbie Williams: English Singer and Songwriter

February 16th – Mahershala Ali: American Actor

February 18th – Jillian Michaels: American Fitness Expert, Nutritionist, Media personality, and Author

February 22nd – James Blunt: British Singer, Songwriter, and Musician

March 5th – Eva Mendes: American Actress

March 24th – Alyson Hannigan: American Actress

April 11th – Tricia Helfer: Canadian and American Actress

April 17th – Victoria Beckham: English Fashion Designer, Singer, and Television Personality

April 28th – Penélope Cruz: Spanish Actress

May 23rd – Jewel: American Singer-songwriter

June 1st – Alanis Morissette: Canadian Singer-songwriter

June 3rd – Kelly Jones: Welsh Singer-songwriter

June 26th – Derek Jeter: Former American Baseball Player, Businessman and Baseball Executive

July 19th – Ramin Djawadi: Iranian-German Film Score Composer, Conductor, and Record Producer

July 28th – Alexis Tsipras: Greek Politician, Former Greek Prime Minister

July 30th – Hilary Swank: American Actress and Film Producer

August 20th – Amy Adams: American Actress

August 31st – Marc Webb: American Filmmaker and Music Video Director

September 19th – Victoria Silvstedt: Swedish Model, Actress, Singer, and television personality

September 19th – Jimmy Fallon: American Comedian, Actor, and Talk Show Host

October 14th – Natalie Maines: American Singer

October 28th – Joaquin Phoenix: American Actor

November 2nd – Nelly: American Rapper and Singer

November 11th – Leonardo DiCaprio: American Actor and Film Producer

December 11th – Rey Mysterio: American Professional Wrestler

December 17th – Sarah Paulson: American Actress

December 21st – Karrie Webb: Australian Professional Golfer

December 24th – Ryan Seacrest: American Media Personality, Game Show Host, and Producer

Deaths (onthisday.com)

January 31st – Samuel Goldwyn: Polish-born Film Producer and Movie Magnate

February 21st – Tim Horton: Canadian Ice Hockey Player and Co-founder of Tim Hortons

February 23rd – Harry Ruby: American Actor, Pianist, Composer, Songwriter and Screenwriter

March 4th – Adolph Gottlieb: American Abstract Expressionist painter, Sculptor and Printmaker

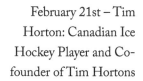

April 2nd – Georges Pompidou: French President and Prime Minister

April 30th – Agnes Moorehead: American Actress

May 13th – Denny Shute: American Professional Golfer

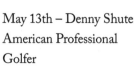

May 24th – Edward "Duke" Ellington: American Jazz Bandleader, Composer and Pianist

June 9th – Miguel Ángel Asturias: Guatemalan Poet-diplomat, Novelist, Playwright and Journalist

June 10th – Prince Henry, Duke of Gloucester: English Prince and Duke

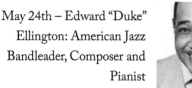

June 22nd – Darius Milhaud: French Composer, Conductor, and Teacher

July 1st – Juan Perón: Argentine Army General and President of Argentina

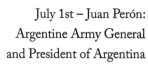

July 9th – Earl Warren: American Attorney, Politician, and Chief Justice of the United States

July 24th – James Chadwick: British Physicist, Discoverer of the Neutron

August 26th – Charles Lindbergh: American Aviator, First to Fly Solo Across the Atlantic

September 21st – Jacqueline Susann: American Novelist and Actress

September 25th – Nicolai Poliakoff: Russian-born, Creator of Coco the Clown

October 9th – Oskar Schindler: German Industrialist, Subject of "Schindler's List"

October 10th – Lyudmila Pavlichenko: Soviet Sniper, Most Successful Female Sniper in History

November 13th – Vittorio de Sica: Italian Film Director and Actor

November 29th – James J. Braddock: American Boxer, World Heavyweight Champion

December 14th – Walter Lippmann: American Writer, Reporter, and Political Commentator

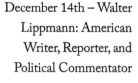

Chapter VII: Statistics 1974

* U.S. GDP 1974 – 1.545 trillion USD (worldbank.org)
* U.S. GDP 2022 – 25.46 trillion USD (worldbank.org)
* U.K. GDP 1974 – 206.1 billion USD (worldbank.org)
* U.K. GDP 2022 – 3.07 trillion USD (worldbank.org)

* U.S. Inflation 1974 – 11.1% (worldbank.org)
* U.S. Inflation 2022 – 8.0% (worldbank.org)
* U.K. Inflation 1974 – 16.0% (worldbank.org)
* U.K. Inflation 2022 – 7.9% (worldbank.org)

* U.S. Population 1974 – 213,854,000 (worldbank.org)
* U.S. Population 2022 - 333,287,557 (worldbank.org)
* U.K. Population 1974 – 56,299,974 (worldbank.org)
* U.K. Population 2022 - 66,971.41 (worldbank.org)

* U.S. Life Expectancy at Birth 1974 - 71.96 (countryeconomy.com)
* U.S. Life Expectancy at Birth 2022 - 79.05 (www.macrotrends.net)
* U.K. Life Expectancy at Birth 1974 – 72.52 (countryeconomy.com)
* U.K. Life Expectancy at Birth 2022 – 81.65 (www.macrotrends.net)

* U.S. Annual Working Hours Per Worker 1974 - 1,844 (ourworldindata.org)
* U.S. Annual Working Hours Per Worker 2017 - 1,757 (ourworldindata.org)

✳ U.K. Annual Working Hours Per Worker 1974 - 1,845 (ourworldindata.org)

✳ U.K. Annual Working Hours Per Worker 2017 - 1,670 (ourworldindata.org)

✳ U.S. Unemployment Rate 1974 – 7.2% (thebalancemoney.com)

✳ U.S. Unemployment Rate 2022 – 3.6% (worldbank.org)

✳ U.K. Unemployment Rate 1974 - 3.7% (ons.gov.uk)

✳ U.K. Unemployment Rate 2022 – 3.7% (ons.gov.uk)

✳ U.S. Tax Revenue (% of GDP) 1974 – 11.8% (worldbank.org)

✳ U.S. Tax Revenue (% of GDP) 2021 – 11.2% (worldbank.org)

✳ U.K. Tax Revenue (% of GDP) 1974 – 23.7% (worldbank.org)

✳ U.K. Tax Revenue (% of GDP) 2021 – 26.4% (worldbank.org)

✳ U.S. Prison Population 1974 - 343,819 (bjs.ojp.gov)

✳ U.S. Prison Population 2021 - 1,204,300 (bjs.ojp.gov)

✳ U.K. Prison Population 1974 - 36,705 (parliament.uk)

✳ U.K. Prison Population 2022 - 81,806 (gov.uk)

✳ U.S. Average Cost of a New House 1974 – $35,900 (gobankingrates.com)

✳ U.S. Average Cost of a New House 2022 – $454,900 (gobankingrates.com)

✳ U.K. Average Cost of a New House 1974 – £10,078 (loveproperty.com)

✳ U.K. Average Cost of a New House 2022 – £296,000 (ons.gov.uk)

* U.S. Average Income per Year 1974 – $11,100 (census.gov)

* U.S. Average Income per Year US 2022 – $56,368 (demandsage.com)

* U.K. Average Income per Year 1974 – £1,997 (gov.uk)

* U.K. Average Income per Year 2022 – £33,000 (gov.uk)

* U.S. Cost of Living: The $100 from 1974 has grown to about $618.88 today, up $518.88 over 49 years due to an average yearly inflation of 3.79%, resulting in a 518.88% total price hike (in2013dollars.com).

* U.K. Cost of Living: Today's £1,333.41 mirrors the purchasing power of £100 in 1974, showing a £1,233.41 hike over 49 years. The pound's yearly inflation rate averaged 5.43% during this period, leading to a 1,233.41% total price rise (in2013dollars.com).

Cost Of Things

United States

* Men's coat, polyester knit, sport: $29.00-$39.00 (mclib.info)

* Women's coat, polyester raincoat: $35.00 (mclib.info)

* Women's handbag: $11.00-$15.00 (mclib.info)

* Fresh eggs (1 dozen): $0.78 (stacker.com)

* White bread (1 pound): $0.35 (stacker.com)

* Sliced bacon (1 pound): $1.32 (stacker.com)

* Round steak (1 pound): $1.80 (stacker.com)

* Potatoes (10 pounds): $1.66 (stacker.com)

* Fresh grocery milk (1/2 gallon): $0.78 (stacker.com)

* Price per gallon: 53 cents (cheapism.com)

* AMC Gremlin: $2,408.00 (mclib.info)

* Men's shirt, acetate sport: $7.99-$10.00 (mclib.info)

* Apples, Washington State: $1.00/3 lbs. (mclib.info)

United Kingdom (retrowow.co.uk)

* Gallon of petrol: 50p

* Bottle of whisky (Haig) (Fine Fare): £2.57

* Pint of beer: 22½p

* Pint of milk: 4½p

* Large loaf of bread: 14½p

* 22" Pye color TV (Currys): £195.00

* 24" Philips black & white TV (Currys): £59.95

* The Daily Mirror newspaper: 3-5p

* ½lb Emblem butter (Tesco): 10½p

* Nescafé 8oz coffee (Tesco): 69p

* Can of Coke (Tesco): 7½p

* Zoppas Fridge-Freezer (Currys): £104.95

* Hotpoint Supermatic twin tub washing machine (Currys): £74.95

* Bendix Autowasher Deluxe automatic washing machine (Currys): £110.00

* One dozen large white eggs: 45p

* 1lb Stork soft margarine (Safeway): 18p

Chapter VIII: Iconic Advertisements of 1974

Budweiser

Converse All Star

Kellogg's Special K

British Airways

Coca-Cola

Toyota '74 Celica GT

Johnnie Walker

Quaker Natural

Tide

Bell Telephone Company

Winchester

United Airlines

Chrysler Dodge

Martini Extra Dry

Kodak Pocket Camera

Virginia Slims

Ford 1974 Thunderbird

Colgate

Smirnoff Vodka

Sony

Campbell's Seashore Soups

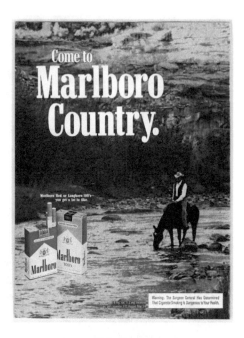

Marlboro

Adidas Baseball Shoes

Camel

General Electric Dispensall Washer

Gordon's Gin

Philips Color TV

I have a gift for you!

Dear reader, thank you so much for reading my book!

To make this book more (much more!) affordable, all images are in black and white, but I've created a special gift for you!

You can now have access, for FREE, to the PDF version of this book with the original images!

Keep in mind that some are originally black and white, but some are colored.

I hope you enjoy it!

Download it here:

bit.ly/3Reen4L

Or Scan this QR Code:

I have a favor to ask you!

I deeply hope you've enjoyed reading this book and felt transported right into 1974!

I loved researching it, organizing it, and writing it, knowing that it would make your day a little brighter.

If you've enjoyed it too, I would be extremely grateful if you took just a few minutes to leave a positive customer review and share it with your friends.

As an unknown author, that makes all the difference and gives me the extra energy I need to keep researching, writing, and bringing joy to all my readers. Thank you!

Best regards,
James R. Miller

Please leave a positive book review here:

amzn.to/3TudpTB

Or Scan this QR Code:

Discover All the Books in This Collection!

Made in United States
Troutdale, OR
06/27/2024

20851421R00060